LEARN TO

L♥VE

YOURSELF

AGAIN

**A Step-by-Step Guide to Conquer Self-Hatred,
Ditch Self-Loathing, & Cultivate Self-Compassion**

Nic Saluppo, M.A.

Table of Contents

Table of Contents

Part II

Part III: Internal Shifts

Table of Contents

Gift

Self-Love Cheat Sheet

Download

Visit
www.nicsaluppo.com/gifts
to download your gift.

In the beginning, these steps won't be natural for you. You'll need something to jolt yourself into remembering them. Without something like that, it'll be too easy to slide back into cycles of self-hatred and loathing, so I've put together a gift for you.

Your cheat sheet comes in two sizes: a standard size and a pocket version. You'll receive both with a single download. With the standard size, you'll get:

- Each of the 6 Steps clearly listed in bold print
- Bullet points refreshing you on how to utilize each step

The standard size is more detailed, but since it's impractical to carry an 8.5 x 11" sheet of paper around with you all day, you'll also get the pocket version, which you simply need to cut out of the larger sheet.

The pocket version is the size of a business card and offers just a few words to remind you of each step. It's sufficient to trigger your memory while still small enough to carry with you anywhere you go. It'll be easy to refer to throughout your day and especially useful if you don't have access to your more detailed sheet. To get your gift so you can use these steps every day, visit:

www.nicsaluppo.com/gifts

Welcome

Welcome. It's an honor to have you here.

Learning to love yourself again (or for the first time) can change everything. It did for me. It changed my relationship with myself, professional life, personal life, and romantic life. It even changed my experience of spirituality.

Experiencing the need to learn to love yourself is normal. When we don't have the know-how to love ourselves, mental illnesses develop. Nobody sets out to purposely not love themselves. We're all doing our best. Unfortunately, our current best is often counterproductive. We essentially reject ourselves, thus creating an internal experience of depression, fear, anxiety, anger, frustration, and so on.

In this book, I'll share my personal journey of going from rejecting and hating myself to loving myself. You'll get the detailed, step-by-step process I used to make that shift. I spent a lot of time and money to learn these steps. Money I could have used to buy a house went toward traveling the US attending workshops and weekly therapy. I'd travel for a week at a time for workshops and drive a 3-hour roundtrip every week from Cleveland, OH to Erie, PA for therapy. It wasn't until I had traveled through the forest and come out on the other side that I looked back and asked, "What worked?" I've taken what worked in learning to love myself and made it into this book.

The world of celebrities is filled with people suffering from anxiety, fear, and depression, all of which are symptoms of not knowing how to love ourselves. Ryan Reynolds, Deadpool; Adele, Someone Like You (1 billion YouTube views); Dwayne Johnson, too many hit movies to count; J.K. Rowling, Harry Potter creator, and so many more have struggled in this way.

I mention these celebrities hoping that you won't view needing to learn to love yourself again as abnormal. Like a pandemic of the soul, this condition runs rampant in our society, and it's a rare individual indeed who never needs help in this area. It's also a rare person who says, *I want to turn my relationship with myself around*. You are one of those rare people, and I'm so excited you're here.

Why This Book?

Uniquely, my life experience affords the ability to write from two perspectives.

The first is from that of someone who has trekked the forest of learning to love myself. The benefit to you is that I've actually been on the trails of mental and emotional pain. Unlike someone who only uses techniques they learned in a textbook, I know where the hills, thorn bushes, and drop-offs are, as well as the spacious and easy trails.

What I've described above is called conscious competence. It's a phrase that refers to a person who has thought deeply about *why* they've succeeded in a certain area and can, therefore, articulate the process to someone else. Unconscious competence is knowing you can do a certain thing while not understanding the process that allows you to do it. It's like a BMX biking video I ordered when I was in middle school.

I was pumped when it arrived because I wanted to be like Ryan Nyquist and learn to do tricks off of dirt jumps. I dreamed of doing a 360 (spinning 360° in the air). Here's what the video said: Go off the jump. Turn your head in the direction you want to spin. Land, and ride away.

Land and ride away? My barely teenage self was crushed. These were the pros, and that's all they could tell me? I now know this was a case of unconscious competence. They could do the trick themselves all day but never thought deeply about their *process* of performing the trick. Don't worry – in this book, I won't be telling you to just "think positive thoughts" or to "chipper up." I've never seen that work. Through thousands of conversations and personal reflections, I intimately understand the process that allowed me to love myself again. I will impart that process onto you in the 6 Steps you'll discover ahead.

The second perspective I have is that of a professional psychotherapist. I guess we got that name as professionals because we have to be a little psycho plus earn a master's degree in mental health counseling. Put them together and you've got a psycho-therapist. So, yeah, I'm one of those. This is your call, but I hope you'll consider my personal journey, of which you'll learn the slimy, grimy details shortly, more important than the fact that I'm a professional psychotherapist.

In my personal journey of learning to love myself, I always sought people out who had "been there." What I wanted to know was, *have you gone on this journey of living with intolerable self-hatred to learning self-love...and not just intellectually learning about it, but experiencing it?* If yes, then I sat at that person's feet (metaphorically) and learned from that person. If not, then I respectfully moved along.

Before learning the concepts in this book, I couldn't comprehend loving myself. I remember being on the phone with one of my mentors, and after 15 minutes of telling him about my emotional pain, we were going to end the call. I said, "Thanks for talking with me," because it was good to be heard and supported by him.

He responded, "Nic, one day you're going to be supporting someone like I'm doing for you."

That was nice of him to say, but at the time I had absolutely no concept of that. I was so deep into self-hatred and loathing I couldn't fathom supporting another person. What did he see that I didn't see? This: That I was working the process. I was sticking with the steps. He knew, like I know about you, that I would get there if I continued following the steps.

Learning to love yourself ("your self") helps you love others. You can only love others to the degree you love yourself.

What to Expect

This is a book of steps. The steps are also tools you can quickly and easily use every day.

In the same way you can't arrive at your target bodyweight and then remain there without some type of maintenance, you can't arrive at loving yourself and then discontinue these steps. Like drinking a cup of water in response to being thirsty, you'll use these steps in response to unpleasant thoughts and feelings.

I recall several pinnacle moments that played a role in learning to love myself. However, there wasn't a singular breakthrough moment when I snapped out of hating myself and began loving myself. Instead, the more habitual these steps became, the more I naturally loved myself.

This book isn't formulated in a "do these steps and then you'll love yourself after the last step" manner, like reaching the top of a staircase and saying, "I'm here." Instead, it's more like a stroll around a beautiful lake where each stride is a step towards loving yourself more deeply. You are inherently loving yourself when you perform any of these steps.

I'm originally from Ohio. There's a beautiful lake in Hinckley, Ohio, called Ledge Lake. Recalling my many visits there, I remember seeing fish in the water, cattails swaying in the wind, a wooden pier large enough for just a few people, rolling hills, sunbathing frogs, and lush, green trees. I'd walk around the lake one day, come back another day, and walk around again. I couldn't get enough of what it offered, and that's what the journey of learning to love yourself is like.

Initially, expect to reach for these tools repeatedly. Soon, because of the changes you'll see in yourself, you'll naturally want to continue using the steps. Over time, you'll no longer need to "reach" for these tools because they'll have become a part of your lifestyle. Since making these steps a lifestyle, my life has become gentle, peaceful, and fluid.

And you'll find 4 Self-Love Experiments peppered throughout this book. These are wonderful opportunities to develop a new type of relationship with yourself: a relationship that involves caring about yourself and getting to know your own heart. Most of us who were emotionally and psychologically abandoned at a young age continue the cycle by abandoning ourselves. The Self-Love Experiments are an opportunity to experience what it's like to be there for *you*.

Last, as a matter of clarity, I'll be referring to feelings and emotions as the same thing. Feelings and emotions are strictly physiological sensations in the body. Feelings aren't thoughts and thoughts aren't feelings. A thought is something you think in your mind while feelings and emotions are physically felt. Grasping this distinction is vital in learning to love yourself, and you'll learn more about it throughout the book.

Notes

Part I

Preface
You Are Elastic

The you who you know is not fixed. You are elastic.

Though you may have come to hate yourself, it doesn't need to remain that way. I've met people from all over the planet who have changed their relationship with themselves. They've gained self-compassion, become gentle on themselves, and started enjoying life. When we're in the thick of not loving ourselves, we think that who we are is fixed. "It's going to be this way the rest of my life." Not true.

You think this because nobody ever taught you how to change. Once you understand how your thoughts and emotions work, you can transform your relationship with yourself. After all, life consists of a series of thoughts and emotions, most of which, until now, have been taking place unconsciously. Your relationship with yourself is determined by how you handle your thoughts and emotions. It's not that you're stuck; it's simply that you didn't know what to do with these parts of yourself.

Self-hatred and suicidal ideation used to be a daily experience for me over a several-year period, and it's amazing to look back and see the changes I've undergone. I didn't change until I met some wonderful people who taught me how to love myself. One of those people was named Ron, and I'm honored that he passed his torch of healing along to me before stepping into eternity. It's a pleasure to share the lessons he taught me with you.

Defining Self-Love

What does it mean to love yourself and have self-compassion?

For perspective, it'll be helpful to look at what it means to not love ourselves. The subtitle of this book mentions self-hatred and loathing, so let's begin there. The self-hatred cycle involves the following:

1. You *notice* something about life doesn't look how you want it to look.

2. You *feel* frustrated that it's not how you want it to be.

3. You *add* harsh self-judgments to the feelings of frustration.

4. The *combination* of judging yourself harshly plus the feelings of frustration results in what we refer to as self-hatred.

Self-hatred, when broken down, is FRUSTRATION + HARSH SELF-JUDGMENTS. You'd think this is about as bad as it can get, but bring in loathing and it gets worse. You're already frustrated, judging yourself, and hating yourself. Then loathing comes in and says, "Oh, and by the way? Things will never, *ever* get better." #OhYay

I was aching for a solution after a 9-year period of living that way. My life had turned upside down and I simply could not figure out how to arrive at a place of loving myself again. How hard did I have to fight my thoughts and emotions to finally win?

Imagine being at a Rose Bowl party and some guy you just met corners you, saying, "I heard you're going through a tough relationship with your dad. You wanna tell me about it?" That was Dan, who, over 11 years later, is still a mentor and dear friend. That was the first time I'd ever had a sense that my feelings were okay just the way they were. It wasn't bad to have feelings; he was actually encouraging me to *share* them. It was the beginning of the breakthrough, which I'm now transmitting to you.

Can you really transmit a breakthrough like that through a book? I hope you'll give me a chance because, not to brag, but I have super-ninja writing skills. It's not a brag at all because these skills developed out of necessity. My normal speaking voice decided to take a hike and never come back many years ago. Life as I knew it would never be the same, and I experienced my world as having been turned upside down. What was once a tool for connection had become a long, exhausting struggle.

It's hard to connect when you can't control your pitch and tone because people don't know how to take what you're saying. They either judge or disengage. With a broken voice, I turned to email as a form of communication. That's how I developed the ability to transmit complex concepts through writing – from years of bypassing the phone and opting to describe things through email. I've landed jobs, entered into relationships, and made deals with new clients all through using the written word as a starting point.

16

This brings us full circle: What does it mean to love yourself? I had to learn to love a person who other people judged and didn't understand. I had to learn to love a person who people thought was drunk, mentally slow, sick, weird, and unrelatable because they didn't know what to make of his voice. Learning to love that person was hard, and I hated myself with a passion for a long time.

I wanted things to go back to the way they were. I wanted my well-functioning voice back. I wish I could tell you that's how it ended up, but it didn't. Speaking is still hard, but the difference is that I embrace who I am with love. I don't fight myself anymore or get caught up in endless cycles of frustration, self-judgment, and self-hatred about my shaky, raspy, breathy, unique voice.

My experience tells me that loving yourself means this: <u>Creating a warm and welcoming environment for all the parts of you which you previously tried fighting, battling, rejecting, avoiding, or pushing away</u>. If you treated another person in those ways, that person would naturally assume you hate them. The same is true when it comes to how you treat parts of yourself. Getting more specific, the "parts" of yourself I'm referring to are your **thoughts** and **feelings**. Consider this: For me, it wasn't my actual voice I hated. Rather, it was the thoughts and feelings I had *about* it.

In reverse engineering self-hatred, we learned that it's a combination of frustration plus harsh self-judgments. If your feelings could dissolve and your thoughts have no impact, it would be very difficult, if not impossible, to hate yourself. You wouldn't have to fight against anything. You'd need only to apply the processes for dissolving feelings and rendering thoughts harmless. Maintaining self-love would then become easy and natural.

The good news is that I learned how to do this, I teach my clients how to do this, and now you will learn how to do this.

Two Prerequisites

Comparing these two prerequisites to learning how to draw makes sense.

If I want to learn pencil drawing, I can read about it. In reading about it, I'll acquire knowledge about it. But if I want to *do* pencil drawing, I'll need a sheet of paper and a pencil. The paper and pencil are the prerequisites for doing pencil drawing.

In the same way, you can learn about loving yourself again by reading these pages. But if you want to experience loving yourself again, you'll need your paper and pencil. Consider these two prerequisites to be your paper and pencil.

Prerequisite One

The first prerequisite is understanding that a lack of self-love is not natural. You weren't inherently made this way.

Before your brain had developed enough to make choices about what to believe or not believe, someone communicated to you through words, facial expressions, or actions that something was wrong with you. The message was that you weren't okay as you were.

By the time you became self-aware enough to think about your thoughts and feelings, this belief that something was wrong with you seemed normal. Just as you never questioned why the hair on your head was there, you never questioned this belief about yourself. It had unconsciously become a part of you, always running in the background.

For example, if you were upset as a child and shamed for it or attention was withdrawn from you, the message was, "There's something wrong with you for being upset." In reality, being upset is a healthy human function, whereas shaming a child for being upset is unhealthy. However, as a baby, infant, or child, you had no concept of that. So, you grew up with the idea that something was wrong with you.

You didn't have the words to describe it because you weren't aware of it, but if you could've had the words, they might've gone something like: "I didn't like how I was treated when I showed my feelings, so I won't show my feelings. I still have feelings, but my caregivers don't like them, so something must be wrong with me because I have so many feelings." Children adapt based on treatment from the caregiver, incapable of questioning whether something is off about the way they are being treated. Given the utter reliance of children on caregivers, losing the caregiver's attention quite literally equals death to the child. Thus, our brains have evolved to unconsciously do whatever it takes, even freezing and blocking our own emotions, to remain in the good graces of our caregivers.

I hope you understand you *learned* to believe something is wrong with you. It isn't natural or inherent. The good news is that since it was learned, it can be unlearned.

Here's the thing I wish you could've known: Whoever taught you that your feelings weren't okay (e.g., *Real boys don't cry* or *it's not ladylike to be angry*) was in truth teaching you how they felt about their feelings. This had nothing to do with you and everything to do with them having rejected their own feelings. They treated your sadness or anger as they treat those emotions in themselves. They couldn't see you as the individual you are because they couldn't see themselves. They could only see they had to shut you down to avoid feeling their own emotions, which were being triggered when they saw you experiencing your emotions. How you were treated is less a reflection of who you are and more a reflection of that person's relationship with themselves.

Now, there's a chance you're like I was in believing you didn't start disliking yourself until later in life due to some event or circumstance. It was the vocal cord issue for me, and you'll hear more about that later. Just know at this point that this issue made it *consciously apparent* that I didn't know how to love myself. Before then, I only thought well of myself because I could "perform." My body did what I wanted when I wanted, but now I couldn't control my voice and suddenly I hated myself. I've realized that if I didn't love myself with a voice condition, then I never loved myself in the first place. It was conditional and performance-based self-love, which isn't love at all.

To summarize the first prerequisite, the belief that something is wrong with you was forced upon you without your consent at an age when you could do nothing about it. (Likely not on purpose, but it happened nonetheless.) By the time you became self-aware, the belief seemed so normal you never questioned it. Since you learned to not love yourself, you can also learn to love yourself.

Prerequisite Two

The second prerequisite is having the mindset that this is not an all-or-nothing situation. You're not going to either always love yourself or never love yourself.

I'd sometimes tell Ron I was completely defeated and discouraged because I had slipped back into old habits of frustration, self-judgment, self-hatred, and loathing. Jokingly, he would say, "I guess all the work you've done up until now has been for nothing!" He had a way of exaggerating what I was thinking and feeling so I could see just how ridiculous it was. In my own mind, it seemed so true. But when blown up times 100, I could see clearly that it wasn't a reliable thought to base my reality upon.

Experiencing a slip back into self-hatred or loathing doesn't mean all is lost and your journey has been useless. View it more in terms of *overall time*. Weather is a good analogy for this.

Personally, I don't like cold weather. My hands get cold and a chill runs down my spine. I'm not a fan of the extra work of packing boots and wearing layers when going somewhere. I don't like scraping ice off my car. I'd rather be hot and sweaty than cold and freezing.

2019-2020 was my first winter living in the deep South and experiencing a mild winter. Most days were in the sixties (Fahrenheit, for those of you reading this in other areas of the world). Every now and then, there was a day in the thirties. When it was 30° outside, do you think I was saying, "Come on! This is useless. I should've stayed up North." No, because I knew I was in a *warm climate*. I felt happy because I knew that soon it would be warm again.

Like the southern climate, loving yourself again isn't all-or-nothing. Overall, it's *so* much better than your old way of life, but there's still going to be a freezing day every now and then. When this happens, take on the mindset that it's okay. Then, continue moving forward with the steps and tools in this book.

To summarize the second prerequisite, don't freak out if you slip back into negativity occasionally. Applying what you learn here is like living in a warm climate of loving yourself. In a climate of self-love there will still be a cold day every now and then. Hanging in there with yourself when you're experiencing challenging or stressful emotions is in itself an act of self-love, as you remained by your own side instead of abandoning yourself.

Quick Summary of Prerequisites

- Not loving yourself was learned, and therefore you can un-learn it.

- Loving yourself isn't all-or-nothing. Stay confident when a cold day comes around.

Introduction

Parma, Ohio.

I'm going 40 in a 25-mph zone and dodging potholes everywhere. Parma has more potholes than every other city in Ohio combined – not joking.

I see lights flashing in my rearview mirror. "Beep!" I yell in my car. Then, "Beep beeping beeper." (When you read *beep*, just imagine the same beeping sound you hear during censored TV shows.)

I was so angry. How dare he pull me over for speeding in an area where I knew exactly what the speed limit was!

"Do you have a radar showing my speed?"

"No, we aren't required by law to catch you on radar."

"Then, I want to take a photo of your radar machine."

"Okay, you're free to do that."

I got out of my car, walked over to the police car and snapped a photo. *That'll surely show him.* I'm embarrassed just writing about the fact that I did this. But it's true. I was *that* guy. That's what self-hatred does. It spews all over into other areas of life. Me speeding and dodging potholes like a maniac? The police officer's fault, of course.

You may be wondering why I was in such a rush. I was heading to work, but before that, I wanted to stop and grab a book I had ordered from the library. I had placed a hold on this book just before it was time to leave for work. The email I received back was, "Your book hold has been received. You can find it on the "Holds" shelf of the library."

Oh good, I thought. *I really don't want to ask the librarian where the book is because of the embarrassing subject matter.*

After receiving my ticket and snapping a photo in the officer's car, I headed to the library. Checking the holds shelf, I saw nothing. Not wanting to ask, I looked for it in the main part of the library based on its number. Still nothing.

~~Very much~~ Desperately not wanting to ask a staff member for the book and hoping I could still find it myself, I looked in both places a second time. Arg. Nothing. If I wanted it right now, which I did, I would have to ask.

"Hi, I placed a book on hold but I'm not seeing it here."

"Oh, okay. I'll look in the back on the cart. It might still be on there."

I could feel the embarrassment building in me because I knew what she would ask next.

"What's the name of the book?"

With my eyes down, I said, "Um, it's called *How to Stop Hating Yourself.*"

Her face communicated both surprise and pity.

That was around eight years ago. I just tried going back to find the book online but didn't see it. All I remember is that it was yellow (75% sure of that) and that I read around only 10 pages (100% sure of that).

I hoped that my self-hatred could be cured by reading pages in a book. I now know that there's only one cure for self-hatred: loving yourself. I'm not talking about loving yourself through forced statements like *I'm awesome!* and *I'm the best!* If you're anything like I was, then someone telling you you're awesome means zilch, and saying it to yourself means less than zilch.

Loving yourself, simply, means *relating* to yourself with love. This is about a relationship with you. The more you treat yourself with love, the less you'll hate yourself. The order of things isn't to first stop hating yourself and then begin treating yourself with love. Treating yourself with love has to come first. Just like ice can't exist in 75° temperatures, neither can self-hatred exist in a climate of self-love.

There are many ways to treat yourself with love. Some of those ways are more effective than others, and what I'd like to do through this book is share with you the ways of treating yourself with love that I, my clients, and my mentors have found to be the most powerful and transformative.

Why I Didn't Love Myself

People list all kinds of reason for not loving themselves. Several common ones are:

- I'm overweight
- I'm too skinny
- I'm too short
- I'm too tall
- I have no money
- People only like me because of my money
- I'm a loser
- I'm not lovable
- I'm not married
- I am married
- My job sucks
- I have no job
- My health is bad
- I'm worried my health will get bad
- Nothing goes right for me
- Now that something is going right for me, I know something will soon go very wrong.

What would you add to the list? Here's how it all started for me.

I developed a voice condition at 19. At first, it wasn't too bad. It would do things like breaking off every now and then and not immediately making the sound I wanted. Generally, I would keep talking and it'd be smooth sailing in just a second.

It got worse after a while. Emotionally, I hung in there for a few months. But, after one too many times of being looked at sideways, awkwardly disengaged with, or outrightly mocked, a new state of mind took hold.

I had previously enjoyed socializing and making new friends through humor and light-hearted interaction. Jokes and anecdotes just aren't as fun or funny when it takes all your effort to simply get the words out. The tone of voice that typically lets people know how to interpret what I was saying was lost. I couldn't simply blurt out a funny Homer Simpson quote because 1) my timing was way off due to the time lapse between thinking about talking and actually making sound, and 2) I couldn't say what I wanted to say in the tone that made it fun to say.

\\\\ \\\\

Attending a little college called Mount Union, I took an awful dive as a junior.

I drove through the beautiful campus, complete with an arching bridge over a little pond. Parking, I stepped out of my car sporting khakis and a stylish black sweater.

My wardrobe was dressy that day because I'd be giving a speech. I walked toward good ol' Chapman Hall, which was not only the oldest building on our campus but in all of Alliance, Ohio. Built in 1864, the men who could spare some of their time during the Civil War had constructed it. As I walked up the stairs into the doorway of a building constructed during a time of war, I knew nothing of the long war that would soon rage within myself.

When it was my turn and I made my way from my desk to the front of the classroom, I was still none the wiser as to what was about to happen and for how long the emotional devastation would last.

`、、、、 、、、、`

As I began reading my paper, I was horrified to find that my voice wouldn't work. In high school, the words on the paper registered in my mind and I simply spoke them in an effortless way. Now, the words were still registering in my mind, but any attempt to vocalize them was met with my vocal cords quickly cutting off or malfunctioning in some other way.

Imagine running a meeting with your associates. You're well acquainted with some and haven't met others until today. As you say *hello*, the "he..." comes out as a deep raspy sound. Then the first "l..." projects up into a high, squeaky pitch while the next "l..." cuts off completely. The "o" sounds like you're blowing wind out of your mouth. Everyone's looking at you with heads tilted to the side. Their eyebrows are contorted into a mixture of confusion and judgment. You try again, but your voice won't make the sound your mind is telling it to make. You know – the same sound you've made millions of times up to this point.

I stumbled through that speech, stunned the entire time over the fact that no matter how much willpower I used, my vocal cords would not make the sounds my mind was telling them to make. I tried so hard to talk that I didn't remember to breathe. The room became a haze and darkness crept in from both sides of my peripheral vision.

On the verge of passing out, I stopped the speech, saying, "Whoa, I feel dizzy." Taking a break to prevent myself from collapsing, I had time to take a few breaths and save myself from a faceplant. At this point, there was dead silence in the classroom. People's jaws were dropped with their eyes wide and fixed intently on me as if to say, *What's going to happen next? Is he going to pass out?*

In addition to being horrified at my voice not working, I also felt utterly humiliated. After crawling through the rest of the speech, I wondered, *What in the world has happened to me?*

\\\\ \\\\

After a few visits with speech pathologists and ENTS, I discovered that I was dealing with mixed type spasmodic dysphonia. With mixed type, sometimes the vocal cords freeze open while other times they freeze shut. A person can also have just one or the other. The freezing of the vocal cords makes it so your voice doesn't produce the sound your mind is telling it to make. Interestingly, Scott Adams, the creator of Dilbert, experienced something similar.

Following the speech incident, I dealt with years and years of being judged, looked at sideways, mimicked and mocked, and awkwardly disengaged with. The sound of spasmodic dysphonia is so unique that most people have no concept of how to interpret it when they hear it. People often think they're dealing with someone who's ill, drunk, or a huge creep. Because of the lack of awareness about this issue in society, people haven't yet learned how to gauge their reactions to someone with a voice that sounds this way.

I took the social rejection hard. Already having been dealing with PTSD before this (unknowingly), now major depression over the loss of being able to control my voice was piled on top. I didn't know how to handle the transition from being a social butterfly and making friends easily to experiencing ongoing judgment and disconnect from people because they didn't know how to react to my voice. I became overwhelmed with frustration and started actively hating myself. Later, you'll see I didn't hate myself for the reason I thought I did. That was a big breakthrough, and I believe it'll be a huge discovery for you, too.

I remember working at a country club one summer. A girl who worked there said, "You should talk more." I took that comment to heart because I *loved* talking and interacting. Contrast that with being in high school and people telling me how "outgoing" I was. An internal battle against depression, PTSD, and my voice issue would roar for nine years. Though the social rejection and misunderstanding was hard, the worst part was dealing with how I felt on the inside. There was a sense of being internally out of control. Was there a way I could love myself under these painful circumstances? (Spoiler alert: yes) I had always relied on the good opinion of others to gauge how I felt about myself. Now, that was no longer a possibility.

I had to either learn to love myself again or die. That's not an exaggeration. Since the speech incident, daily life had become so miserable that I was thinking about suicide regularly. Before experiencing this inner pain, I couldn't understand why people would ever consider suicide. It's never about selfishness; it's about wanting to *escape* the prison of your own mind and body. If your body is the prison, there's nowhere to go. If your own mind tortures you, where can you hide?

The only way out of such a prison is doing a complete remodel. Bring in the remodelers, have them tear down the prison and rebuild a welcoming home. The steps in this book are about creating a welcoming home inside of you.

With each consecutive step, I'll explain exactly what to do so you can learn to love yourself again. Along the way, I hope you'll take time to pause and look around – there's more beauty and wonder waiting for you than you can imagine.

Notes

_____

_____

_____

_____

_____

_____

_____

_____

_____

_____

_____

_____

Part II

Step 1

The Double Arrow
Stop Fighting Against Yourself

"What you resist not only persists, but will grow in size." -Carl Jung

B efore learning the steps in this book, I would often get into a tizzy about my life. A particular instance from about eight years ago comes to mind.

It started with me wishing I had more money. That led to feeling anxious and fearful about finances. That led to judging myself and beating myself up internally about not having more money. That led to stomping around the house with my palms open and shaking my arms up and down, saying, "I can't believe it. I can't believe this is my life. This is my life! Ah!"

To be clear, I wasn't saying that in a happy way. I was saying it in the worst way possible, as in, "I hate the fact that this is my life." Now, it might be funny to see the whole thing on video. However, I was an enormous mess on the inside at the time. It seemed I couldn't pivot, maneuver, be mentally elastic, or emotionally agile. Call it whatever you want, but I didn't know how to do it.

I'd get myself into crazy mental and emotional messes so quickly because I would automatically Double Arrow myself without knowing I was doing it. I'd think about finances and wish I had more money, which is not ideal but still okay. Then, I'd feel a bit stressed over wishing I had more money. Also not ideal, but this wasn't enough to bring about stomping around and waving my hands. The next step brought on the prancing and waving.

I would then feel angry, upset, frustrated, afraid, anxious, and ashamed over the fact that I was feeling stressful emotions. That's what brought it on.

To recap, I felt stressed. Next, I felt stressed *about* feeling stressed. That was the tipping point, and that's what the Double Arrow is.

37

During this situation, I remember thinking thoughts like, "I hate myself and I hate my life." Not being aware of the Double Arrow when it happens makes it all too easy to fall into a bottomless pit of negativity.

\\\\ \\\\

Being aware of Double Arrows is the first step for loving yourself again. I see people fall into emotional oblivion all the time due to a lack of awareness. In the above example, I had no power over my emotions because I didn't know it was happening. Repeatedly, I teetered from an illusion of stability and happiness to becoming overwhelmed with negativity.

The key is to not resist the initial upset. You're upset about something? Okay. Sure, it's not ideal, and we will absolutely address it later in this book, but for now, let it be okay to be upset. Being upset about money, relationships, a health issue, yourself in general, or whatever it may be isn't where you want to remain. On the flip side, it's leaps and bounds better to be in that space for a little while than being upset plus being upset *about* the fact that you're upset.

One is a singular problem which you can address, but the other is a problem sandwich. Now you're dealing with the original issue plus the fact that you're upset about being upset. When you serve yourself a problem sandwich, that's when things get dicey. By resisting the initial upset, you've enlarged the *overall* upset.

Let's look at how to use your Double Arrow Shield so you can deflect it before it ever takes hold.

The Double Arrow Shield

You'll go through a 3-part process to complete this step and use the Double Arrow Shield. All three parts take place only in your mind and body, so the entire process can be completed in a matter of seconds.

Part 1: Be aware.

Part 2: Let it be okay.

Part 3: Relax your body.

Part 1: Be aware.
The sooner you're aware of being upset, the sooner you can cease resisting it. Remember, resisting the initial upset causes more overall upset. With my voice, I'd become very upset when it wouldn't work properly, which was many times per day.

First, I'd be upset it wasn't working properly, then upset I had dysfunctional vocal cords, then think about how badly that sucked. I'd end up in a crisis about how my entire life was a terrible mess. In a matter of seconds, I was drowning in self-hatred while loving myself was 100 miles in the opposite direction. Resisting the initial upset leads to subsequent upsets, which are what lead to self-hatred and not loving yourself. Simply be aware of the initial upset as you would be aware of seeing a chipmunk running over a log.

Part 2: Let it be okay.
Now that you're aware of the upset, it's time to consciously give it

meaning. Until now, you've unconsciously given it meaning. The new, conscious meaning is: *It's okay*.

Today, when my voice doesn't make the sound I had intended, I'm simply aware of it. I let it be okay because I know there will be more stress if it's not okay.

Letting it be okay is inherently loving yourself. When it's not okay, who or what are you fighting? Yourself. Fighting yourself is the opposite of loving yourself. Just like it's okay that the chipmunk runs across a log, it's okay that feelings are taking place inside of you.

Part 3: Relax your body.
Relaxing your body gives the upset feelings more space. If I confine the chipmunk in a small container, how many times will it run back and forth? Probably again and again nonstop because it can't find a way out. Unconfined, it runs over the log once and you don't see it again. Confining your emotions creates more density and intensity, causing you to feel worse.

When my voice doesn't make the sound I'm shooting for, after I've become aware and let it be okay, I then relax and let the upset feeling do what it wants. When I resisted this, I would find myself in 30-day (plus!) battles against my feelings, always resulting in utter exhaustion. Now, I easily relax my body – forehead, jaw, shoulders – and let the feeling do what it wants. It typically sputters around for a few seconds and then it's gone.

The Psychological Mechanism Behind
The 3-Part Process

This boils down to the concept of underlying meanings.

For example, if someone says to you, "Even you should be able to figure this problem out," there's an underlying meaning beneath the words. Specifically, the underlying message is, "I think you're dumb, but this problem is so easy that even someone who is dumb should be able to figure it out." This begs the question: What underlying meaning are you communicating to yourself when an upset feeling isn't okay? There are two layers.

First, if it's not okay, then that implies there's something *wrong* with it.

Second, if there's something wrong with the feeling, then there's something wrong with you, as you're the one experiencing the feeling.

By not letting the initial upset be okay, it's as if you're speaking an underlying message to yourself that you as a person are not okay. That explains why resisting the feeling is a precursor to thoughts of self-hatred; resisting the feeling, i.e., not letting it be okay, is an unconscious act of self-hatred. Not resisting the feeling is a precursor to thoughts of self-encouragement, because not resisting is an act of self-love.

Quick Review

- Double Arrowing yourself means being upset *about* being upset.

- Instead of resisting the initial upset, use the Double Arrow Shield:

  - Be aware: Notice the initial upset.

  - Let it be okay: Avoid telling yourself the feeling is unacceptable.

  - Relax your body: Density creates emotional intensity, and relaxation creates emotional space and ease.

- Letting the feeling be okay is an act of self-love because you're no longer battling against yourself.

Self-Love Experiment #1
Do Something Kind for Yourself

Do this by making yourself a promise and following through on that promise. For example, you can promise yourself a walk on a trail you like or a few hours of fishing at your favorite spot. If it would be fun to get ice cream or go bowling, you can promise that to yourself. It could also be a massage, seeing an old movie you enjoyed while growing up, or finally trying the dance lessons you've been interested in. Whatever it is, make sure you set a specific day and time with yourself.

To ensure you strengthen trust, love, and compassion with yourself, following through is vital. Nobody likes it when someone says, "Yeah, I'll be there," and then they don't show up. Just the same, your psyche doesn't like it when you do this to yourself. Remember, you're creating a new, loving relationship with you. Make following through as important as showing up to your wedding or being someone's ride to a job interview.

Keep in mind that this experiment isn't about gorging or finding a reason to splurge. It's also not about hiding from your feelings through an activity, food, or anything else. This experiment is about taking a moment to bring your attention to your heart, asking, "What would be exciting, fun, or meaningful to me?"

I once rented the 1992 *3 Ninjas* movie in my early thirties because some part of me thought it would be fun to watch. When you do something like this, think of it as both doing a kind favor *for* a loved one and gratefully receiving a kind favor *from* a loved one.

Self-Love Experiment #1, Continued
Do Something Kind for Yourself

Keeping your promise to yourself moves you towards wholeness, just as keeping a promise to a loved one, friend, or client builds trust with that person.

Notes

Step 2

Healthy Physical Habits
The 4 Cornerstones

"In fact, rest is a critical component of achieving
sustainable excellence over time." -Tony Schwartz
(Quote taken from *Maximize Your Potential*, by Jocelyn K. Glei)

Since the introduction and first step were more about your state of mind, the second step will be about physical action steps.

In thinking back to the days before learning to love myself, it's clear anybody could see I didn't love myself based on my habits. I would fall asleep on the couch with the TV on, then get up at 2:00 am and go to bed. I wasn't eating regularly. I'd go out on a day trip and not bring any food, becoming hangry within a couple of hours.

I remember a phone conversation with Ron about how frustrated and pissed off I was. I had just spent the day at the river trying out my new hobby of fishing for steelhead. It could've been a fun day, except I rushed in the morning and didn't eat much or drink enough water. Soon, I was hangry (if you haven't heard the term "hangry," it's a state of being angry and hungry).

I had trekked through the woods and sat out there hungry and thirsty only to catch nothing. Now, I was driving home in a terrible mood.

"You're spiraling downward," Ron said. "And I bet you haven't eaten enough."

Funny. I didn't tell him that. How did he know?

He had been around long enough to know that people who don't love themselves treat themselves physically as if they don't love themselves.

〃〃〃 〃〃〃

Here's a helpful perspective to consider this from: What if there was a person following you around all the time? Like Tails in the Sonic video games. Tails just shows up. Except, your person isn't a helper like Tails is to Sonic.

This person blocks the faucet so you can't drink water. You have a water bottle, but every time you attempt to drink, they slap it out of your hand. They don't let you eat, either. You make a nice meal and they toss it in the trash. You're sleepy, but they blast loud music so you can't fall asleep. You try and use the bathroom, but they lock the door so you can't get in, and now you've got to hold it.

That's essentially what I was doing to myself. In my professional work and through simply observing others, it's clear this is a common pattern of people who haven't learned to love themselves.

People who love themselves use the 4 Cornerstones of healthy physical habits:

1. Go to the bathroom when nature calls
2. Eat when they're hungry and plan ahead to make sure they'll have enough to eat for the day
3. Stay hydrated with plenty of water
4. Let their bodies rest

\\\\ \\\\

When you've got to use the bathroom and you don't do it, your organs down there are under immense strain. You may not be consciously aware of it, but they're feeling it. It's a concrete act of self-love to make time to use the restroom.

How often do you find yourself hangry? Or, maybe not hangry specifically, but still hungry? Having been an exercise scientist in my previous career, I can tell you that your body breaks down its own muscle and uses it for fuel in these situations. Especially when you're physically active, your body needs fast-acting fuel. You won't just burn fat, because fat isn't a fast-acting energy source. When your body needs something quicker and you haven't eaten, it'll break down muscle and burn that for energy. It's a concrete act of self-love to eat when (or before) you're hungry. (On the other extreme, I'm not saying to constantly overeat) Additionally, it's an act of self-love to plan what, when, and where you will eat if you know you will be out for the day.

I'm adding this paragraph several weeks after having the book professionally edited and the final copy completed. Having taken up intermittent fasting over the last few days, I think it's worth noting. I've been doing a 16-hour fast and eating two larger meals within an 8-hour window. Normally, I wouldn't include something like this after just a few days of experimentation, but my results are worth noting:

- No hanger

- No grumbly stomach

- Lessened desire for a midday nap

- No tiredness after meals

- Stable blood sugar levels

- High, consistent energy levels

- Ability to do aerobic and bodyweight exercises with just as much, if not more, energy. This is true even after 12-16 hours of fasting (no heavy weight training). I'm writing this after having mowed the lawn with a push mower for one hour in 96° heat and having fasted for 15.5 hours. I feel excellent.

- I'm not sure what I weighed before starting, but I've definitely leaned down by what looks to be around 3-4 pounds.

This is much different than the typical three square meals per day approach with snacks between meals. I'm so shocked at my results that I thought it worthwhile to include this information here. Having only done this for a few days, I don't know enough to make final conclusions. This is not an advertisement for intermittent fasting – this is simply me telling you what my experience has been for the purpose of giving balance and a differing perspective about eating habits.

''''' '''''

How about water and hydration? We can spend an entire book describing the healthy effects ample water has on you and the negative impacts of low water intake. Just to list a few, hydration plays a huge role in A) brain function (do you have brain fog?) B) carrying nutrients to cells, and C) removing waste from cells.

Even when you're sleeping or not thinking intensively, the brain still needs plenty of hydration to bring nutrients in and waste out because it remains active. Water is the medium through which that happens. The more well-hydrated you are, the more easily your body can function optimally.

Think of hydration and your brain in terms of Play-Doh. Imagine opening a fresh container of your favorite Play-Doh color. It's soft and you can easily form it into any shape.

Later, someone comes by and uses it, forgetting to seal the lid afterward. D'oh! By the time you use it again, it's a bit dried out. Not unusable, but it doesn't move as easily and you can feel the dryness in your hands.

Just as slightly dried out Play-Doh still functions, a slightly dehydrated body will still function. However, from the perspective of your hands touching the Play-Doh, it doesn't move as easily. The same is true from the perspective of your veins and arteries for pumping nutrients to your brain and clearing out waste. If they could talk, your blood vessels would say, "We can still get the job done, but it's much easier for us when we have plenty of water!"

\\\\ \\\\

Last but not least, rest. We're going to spend more time on this subject because the concept of rest is shrouded by guilt and shame for many of us. We were trained to believe that resting is bad by people who didn't know how to love themselves. You are only valuable when you're being productive, efficient, and getting things done, so goes the belief. Get anything done, really. Just stay busy and do *something*. So, instead of enjoying a beautiful bench overlooking the lake, you opt to organize that corner of the garage. Our garage does have a special corner in need of some organizing.

Learning to base your sense of value on productivity alone, the underlying message is that you have to pick between two options:

1. Stay busy, or 2. Tell yourself you're a lazy piece of garbage while attempting to rest. Maybe you try kicking your feet up, but all you can think about are the things you "should" be doing.

Ron noticed that I had difficulty resting without guilt, saying, "Don't be afraid to put your feet up and relax." *Huh? Really?* I had no idea that was even an option. Can people do that without being lazy?

I tried it out. Having direct permission from Ron to not beat myself up over it, I didn't judge myself as lazy. Wow. What an experience. They say your first kiss is a huge deal, but no, no, no. It's your first time experiencing guilt-free relaxation that is a true thing of wonder.

I felt the cushion on the couch supporting my back and the footrest supporting my feet (okay, fine, I admit it…I was 25 and it was a futon in our bachelor pad, not a couch). I noticed the sensation of taking the weight off my legs because, for the first time, I was present with relaxing. But that wasn't the best part. It was the release of mental and emotional tension that comes from relaxing with no self-judgment. For the first time, my mind could turn off completely or just look around spontaneously and enjoy what it saw.

People who can't relax and always have to be busy aren't the people you want to be learning from. A compulsion to be constantly busy is a sign of a lack of inner peace. Were they to slow down, it would be more uncomfortable than staying busy. Being busy is what covers up their lack of inner peace.

Truly productive people know the importance of rest and relaxation. Elite performers alter between productivity and rest. It's a researched subject (see K. Anders Ericsson's violinist study). Rest increases productivity. Relaxation fuels the quality of the activity. Without it, the activity would be mediocre. In *The Last Dance*, a documentary about Michael Jordan and the 1998 Chicago Bulls, Jordan says, "It's good our coach let us have the day off to rest and relax. A younger coach would have had us practicing today. Coach knows we need to relax." MJ and the head coach, Phil Jackson, both understood the value of rest. A lack of rest does not lead to better productivity; it acts to cover up the feelings of guilt and shame one feels when not being busy.

Brian Johnson, creator of Philosophers Notes, wrote that he has a daily routine of starting his day around 3:30 am, meditating and napping around 7:30 am, and then doing another few hours of focused work. If businesses wanted to get the most out of their employees, they would offer a 90-minute lunch break with cots available so staff could eat and nap. The quality of work during the second half of the day skyrockets after a short rest. The tradeoff would be 2.5 hours less on the clock per week for each employee in exchange for increased work quality.

When I started writing, I would try to push through finishing sections of a book. Clearly, I was tired. I'd consider the possibility of lying down for an hour and then finishing up, but mental resistance quickly came in. "You're lazy if you take a rest," one part of my mind would say.

Well, I don't like that, I'd think in response. *I'll keep pushing through.*

"Wait a minute," a third, wiser part of me chimed in. "Resting doesn't make a person lazy. If rest is for the purpose of avoiding work, then sure, keep working. But I clearly want to do this work, and I trust myself to complete it after an hour of rest. In fact, the quality and focus of my work will have increased."

Discovering this distinction between resting to avoid work vs. trusting myself to return to the work after resting was huge in the quest to love myself. When earning my bachelor's degree, I avoided schoolwork like kids avoid broccoli. "No!" I would say in my mind. "I don't wanna." Then my mind would cross its arms and go play video games or hang out with friends. Seriously, though, I played a ton of Mortal Kombat Trilogy on N64 with my housemates while rocking a D average in organic chemistry. So, I retook the course. Naturally, I got an A. No, no I didn't. I got another D. Side note: After also having no interest in inorganic chemistry, I dropped the course of study altogether and studied psychology instead.

Knowing I could avoid work just because I didn't want to do it, I grew to distrust myself. "Oh, you're tired? Too bad, finish writing the book now!" I began trusting myself again once I saw that I could take time to rest and then get back to work with no problem.

Resting: It's not inherently lazy. If your brain or body is tired, resting is healthy. It's a way of loving yourself. Sometimes, when there's something I want to avoid, I'll get busy doing something else. *Look at me, I'm organizing the special corner in the garage* (to avoid going grocery shopping). *Hey, this is great, I'm mowing the lawn* (to avoid writing my psychotherapy session notes).

To summarize, our brains and bodies are made to require rest. When your motive is to avoid something, resting can be sneaky. However, when used in a healthy way, it's a great source of rejuvenation and enjoyment as well as a means for increasing focus and quality of work.

\\\\ \\\\

Here's how you can implement the 4 Cornerstones into your life:

Cornerstone 1: Evacuation

Some people are so busy they don't make time to evacuate waste from their bodies. I knew an individual who once bragged about getting bladder and urinary tract infections due to working long hours without a break. It's not supposed to stay in there, which is why it's called waste. When you don't evacuate it out of you, it's toxic to your bowels and urinary system, making going to the bathroom an act of self-love.

This requires just a bit of body-awareness. Simply bring your awareness to the lower gut and hip area every hour. Don't wait until you have to go so badly that something's about to burst.

Cornerstone 2: Fuel

What kind of fuel does your body need? I find that avocados, eggs, and oatmeal with peanut butter provide the fuel I need for long stretches of focused work. Those foods are also good for jogs and other forms of cardio exercise. On the other hand, I feel better if I've eaten some carbohydrates when doing more intense exercise.

It helps if you have a grocery store ritual. Every, say, Tuesday evening, you go to the grocery store. Even if you're not completely out of food, this weekly trip will ensure you have the right foods to maintain a regular eating schedule. Getting 80% of the same foods each week makes it easy to plan meals and prevents you from getting into a situation where you don't have enough food to take with you for the day. Being hangry is an unpleasant experience, and it can be prevented by having a shopping routine.

Cornerstone 3: Hydration
Purchase a single 40 oz water bottle. Make sure it's clear. Using tape or a marker, split it into five even sections. Each section will be 8 oz each, as 8 oz x 5 = 40 oz. Drink 8 oz out of a glass when you wake up. Then take the bottle with you for the day, drinking 8 oz every 2-hour period. I like to evaluate my urine as the day goes. If it's a bit yellow, I'll drink more. Nice and clear, I know I'm well-hydrated.

Cornerstone 4: Rest
If you can swing it, a power nap between clients or during your lunch break will do wonders. I used to take a power nap in my car if I had a moment between clients during my personal training days. As an intern counselor, I'd do the same thing before seeing a block of clients later in the day. 20 minutes is best, but just 5-10 minutes can refresh your brain.

With a regular sleeping schedule, a pre-bed routine is the most important factor. Your body will respond to the routine and know it's time to begin slowing things down. Reading in bed, meditating, or having prayer time are all great routines. The first few nights may not make a difference, but soon, like Pavlov's dogs salivated for food when they heard the bell, your brain will "salivate" for sleep when you engage in the routine. I can't emphasize how much better you'll feel maintaining a regular sleeping schedule rather than finding yourself on the couch at 2:00 am because you fell asleep watching TV like I used to do.

The Psychological Mechanism Behind
The 4 Cornerstones of Healthy Physical Habits

You might think the way you treat yourself is irrelevant, but part of you notices. How you feel about yourself, then, is largely based on how you treat yourself. Thinking back to the example of imagining someone following you around not allowing you to eat, drink, sleep, or go to the bathroom, you can clearly see how you would [quickly] grow to hate such a person. When that person is you doing it to yourself, you then quickly grow to hate yourself.

Not providing yourself time for the 4 Cornerstones of healthy physical habits will cause a subtle shift in your mind that you must not care for yourself very much. When this behavior is continued, it won't be so subtle. At least, that's my experience.

Conversely, taking time for the 4 Cornerstones will create a subtle shift that you care for and love yourself. Soon, the unconscious parts of your psyche will see the consistency and form a newfound confidence in your ability to love yourself. The confidence dissolves much of the inner anxiety you previously had. The 4 Cornerstones are so concrete and simple to implement, they act as an excellent slingshot into the upcoming steps that will permanently transform your mental and emotional health.

Consider that the 4 Cornerstones create a sense of stability in your life — something you've likely been missing — allowing you to approach the upcoming internal shifts with a sense of security.

Quick Review

The 4 Cornerstone Physical Habits are:
1.   Evacuation
2.   Fuel
3.   Hydration
4.   Rest

Evacuation: When you don't evacuate, it means you're holding toxic waste in your body. Get that stuff outta there!

Fuel: Regular meals each day and a ritual of going to the store each week will help you avoid the hangry attacks.

Hydration: Blood flows more easily with ample hydration. Improved blood flow means more easily bringing nutrients to your cells and clearing the leftover toxins away. Use a 40 oz water bottle with marked lines at 8 oz intervals.

Rest: Ensure a regular sleep schedule by utilizing a pre-bed routine. It's optional, but a power nap can provide a much-needed boost if you can find the time and a place to take one.

Notes

Part III

Internal Shifts to Love Yourself

Introduction to Internal Shifts

You battle and strive to repress your feelings because you think they'll never go away. In this section, you will learn that the opposite is true. The *less* you battle and repress your emotions, the *faster* they go away. Anyone who's fighting against their feelings is in for a long, fatiguing battle.

Before learning to mentally and emotionally deal with the fact that my voice no longer functioned as it used to, I'd get very upset over it, sending myself into a multi-day train ride directly to Crazy Town. Having learned and used the steps in this part of the book allows me to effortlessly rise above and move on from the [many] moments when my voice doesn't function properly. Contrast that with when I was in middle school and into BMX biking. I wanted to show my mom and sister how high I could jump my bike off a wooden ramp.

I was a little irked when I didn't have a great first attempt. When the second attempt also didn't work out, and having no concept of how to dissolve emotions, frustration overtook me. I shoved the bike and it went for a 30-yard ghost ride, eventually being stopped by the basement window it crashed into. The bike taking on a life of its own and smashing into the window is a great image for how we end up when we don't know what to do with overwhelming emotions.

Processing emotions is a physical need just like going to the bathroom. Once you grasp that, you'll have more of a willingness to take time for yourself in that area instead of shoving the feelings down repeatedly. The "hold it in" method certainly doesn't work with our bladder and bowels.

Learning to be with your feelings in a healthy way is like going on a journey with someone, except that someone is yourself. In *The Lord of The Rings* movie series, Frodo and Sam traveled long and far together, forming a deep, close friendship by the end. Taking time to be with your feelings in a constructive way leads to developing depth, closeness, and intimacy with yourself.

Step 3

The Observation Solution
Rendering Negative Thoughts Harmless

"Thoughts are not the problem. Believing them is." -Byron Katie

dentifying with your thoughts will get you into trouble. The solution is to observe them, which we'll call The Observation Solution.

With my vocal cord issue, I used to think of myself as a freak. Not in a good way as in, *He's a freak on the court!* This was more like, *I'm a freak who people are repelled by.*

When my voice didn't come out how I intended during conversation, all the worst-case scenario alarms in my brain would go off. *Alert! YOU ARE A FREAK. Alert! YOUR LIFE SUCKS.*

Believing the alarming thoughts, I would think, "Oh, no. This is just terrible. It's absolutely terrible." I would then feel anxious, afraid, and frustrated in the worst way possible. After all, my mind was *telling me* I was a freak. If my mind says so, then it's true. Right?

The Observation Solution comes at this point in the process because, next, you'll learn to use the power of observation to untangle your thoughts and feelings. When thoughts and feelings become enmeshed or blended with one another, it creates an emotional disaster. Separating thoughts from feelings is the silver bullet of this book. But without first developing an ability to observe your thoughts, you won't be able to utilize the silver bullet. Think of your capacity to observe your thoughts rather than identify with them as the gun that holds the silver bullet. You could just skip ahead and take the bullet, but you can't fire it without a gun.

Thoughts aren't a big deal. No, really, they aren't. Most people think their thoughts are who they are. In reality, your mind (i.e., the producer of your thoughts) is a tool for you to use to live a fulfilling life. Think about hitting a nail with a hammer. Sometimes you don't hit the nail on the head, and sometimes you do. Frankly, it doesn't matter if you miss a couple of times.

If the nail bends, you can simply pull it out and start over with a new nail. Missing a couple of times isn't a terrible thing; just reset and fire off another whap of the hammer. Even Thor, with his all-powerful hammer, misses sometimes. Were you to miss 10 or 20 times, or more, it's likely that the nail will still end up where you want it, which is with the head flush against the board you're pounding it into.

Now, when you misfire with the hammer and don't hit the nail precisely on the head, do you throw the hammer and toss your arms up? "I am a complete nail-misser! I'll never pound that nail in!" Probably not. You just reset and strike again.

Like the hammer, your mind is a tool. Sometimes it misfires, but it's simply a tool, so it's up to you to reset it and strike again. The issue comes when you identify with your thoughts, believing they are who you are. When this happens, you get negative very fast.

"I'm a loser." There's someone on social media I know who posts that about himself every few months. I'm concerned for him because he's identifying with his thoughts. There's no escape route as long as he continues identifying with his thoughts.

Anybody might have a thought of being a loser. The difference is, do you take it as absolute truth or view it as a misfire, quickly resetting and moving forward?

Everybody experiences negative thoughts about themselves. I remember reading a story about a top-level public speaker. He shared that after decades of experience, he would still throw up before each speech. He'd then walk onto the stage and deliver a killer speech. There's an important lesson in that.

Just because you have a thought that you're a loser one second doesn't mean you can't continue moving forward with the goal that means the most to you the next second. Thoughts are not truth. You might think they're truth, but thinking so has nothing to do with reality. Thinking your thoughts are truth is yet *another* thought you've identified with. Here are a few thoughts I've had that ended up not being true:

1. At 10 years old, I thought I would *never* score a goal in soccer. I'd been playing for four years and hadn't scored a single one. I remember crying in the car after another game of not scoring a goal. Later that season I scored a few goals and became a leading scorer in subsequent seasons.

2. For a long time, I thought I'd never get married. I was disturbed about it, too. I remember yelling at God about it. Nick Vujicic, born with no arms and no legs, thought the same thing about himself. "Who would want to marry someone with no arms or legs?" He did get married, and in one of his books, wrote, "If you think you're called to marriage, don't give up on it. God has someone for you." I thought he was completely full of $h*t. Well, it took going on a lot of dates and meeting a lot of people, but I met someone who shares my values of faith and personal growth. I often contemplate that I spent so many years be-

ing upset because my thoughts told me there was nobody like my wife out there, when in fact, she existed all along.

3. I thought I would never get over major depression. Having lived with it for nine years, I was certain it was a permanent fixture in my life. I was so certain of this that I thought about suicide regularly. Well, here I am, having been off psychotropic medications for 11 years and free of depression for nine years. I don't say that intending to brag; rather, to infuse hope into you. My journey of emotional healing is why I'm an author and psychotherapist today. I am so utterly grateful to have discovered that *the way out is through*, and I think it's worth sharing with others also dealing with hopelessness.

Given the examples above, you can see why I say thoughts aren't a big deal. They're not. They don't determine reality. After having had my thoughts proven wrong time after time, I now see my mind in a new light. It's a tool to make use of, not my identity. (for a brief discussion on identity, see Appendix A)

\\\\ \\\\

I know someone who, if he can't immediately win at something or do it well, he gets angry, frustrated, throws his hands up, and quits. This is a smart and talented person with lots of potential. The issue is that he feels an initial burst of frustration, attaches self-judgment onto the frustration, and the combination of the two leads to him having difficulty trying and enjoying new experiences.

When it comes to writing this book, the thought *you're never going to finish* has popped into my mind a few times. Given my experience of seeing that thoughts aren't based on any reality other than the wacky and wild mind of Nic, which isn't reality at all, the thought of not finishing does not affect me. Using The Observation Solution, I simply notice the thought in my mind and then it blows away like a leaf in the wind. I then continue utilizing my mind as a tool to accomplish my goal of finishing this book.

Here's something to consider: Where did you get the idea that you *have to* believe your thoughts in the first place? Learning to love yourself is very difficult when you think you must believe every thought you have. One second, you're totally awesome and the coolest person alive. Then, you're a less-than-human, complete and utter loser the next. That's what happens when you believe your thoughts. The mind is a tool, so don't use it to give yourself an identity. Instead, use it to pursue things that are meaningful to you.

\\\\ \\\\

At the beginning of this step, I shared that my internal alarms would go off when my voice didn't work properly, which was hundreds of times per day. Eventually, I learned to stay calm. "Oh, look. I see that I'm judging myself. Interesting. Moving on..." Observation of my thoughts allowed me to remain calm and prevented me from identifying with them.

It's like your thoughts say, "Hey sexy thang, wanna go for a ride with me?" I used to get in the car every. Single. Time.

I started saying, "Thanks for the offer, but I'll pass."

To be clear, my voice still breaks up hundreds of times per day. It can be physically difficult. However, it doesn't need to be physically *and* emotionally difficult. I reset and take another swing hundreds of times per day, confident that the nail will eventually end up flush with the wood. And it always does.

῁῁῁ ῁῁῁

Observing your thoughts is quite simple, requiring just one step. The difficulty arises in *remembering* to do it.

If you're used to identifying with your thoughts, it can seem like quite a task to not do so. Here's the simple thing about it – you don't have to do anything beyond observing. There's no 3-part process and nothing else to remember. As soon as you say, "Oh, look, I notice I'm thinking judgmental thoughts again," you've completed this step and used this tool. I recommend using that exact phrase: Oh, look, I notice I'm thinking..."

As simple as it sounds, remembering to do this can be difficult because you've never questioned whether your thoughts were true. You may need to catch yourself in the middle of a ride to Crazy Town a few times. Soon, you'll catch yourself before boarding the train.

At the beginning of this book, I said that I'm someone who has trekked through the woods of learning to love myself again. I'll offer an important trail-tip right now, and I hope you'll consider it on the same level as being told where an enormous drop-off cliff is on the trail. If you can remember this, you'll be golden. It's this: Emotions make your thoughts believable. If you have the thought,

I'm a loser, and then you're flooded with anxiety, fear, sadness, and frustration, the unpleasant way your body feels will reinforce the thought. You'll assume the thought is true because your body feels so physiologically awful when you think it. This information gives you permission to not believe your thoughts even when there are a few emotions to go along with them.

Because the emotions associated with thoughts can be intense, you may need a reminder to observe your thoughts instead of believing them. A bracelet or an alarm on your phone could both work. You might also consider printing out the business card-sized PDF gift offered at the beginning of this book and taping it to a piece of cardboard and keeping it in your pocket.

Life will become much easier when you stop battling or judging your thoughts and begin observing them.

The Psychological Mechanism Behind
The Observation Solution

Observing your thoughts creates an immediate increase in your ability to love yourself. It does this by stopping the impending avalanche of subsequent thoughts and emotions before they have a chance to build momentum.

A singular thought is no problem. However, once a few emotions and a long series of thoughts are added to the mix, things get messy and fast. It's like trying to outrun an avalanche in 3-feet of snow. The snow actually makes the avalanche itself move faster while simultaneously slowing you, the person running away from it, down. By developing a keen eye for what gets an avalanche started in the first place, you can choose a different route before it's too late.

Psychologically speaking, thoughts lead to emotions and emotions lead to worse, more hopeless thoughts, which then lead to even more intense emotions. Soon, you're doing the stomp-and-prance dance around your house like me all those years ago.

Don't make your mind something it's not supposed to be. It's not meant to give you a sense of identity, purpose, or meaning. As discussed, it's a tool for pursuing the things you choose to pursue.

The common idea that self-esteem must be derived from thinking thoughts like, *I'm awesome!* is not helpful. I'm neither awesome nor unawesome. I simply am. It's okay to just be. I make decisions about what to use my mind for and then I do those things. But I avoid placing judgments on myself by labeling myself as better or worse, greater or lesser, above or below, awesome or loser, and so on.

Simply notice your thought and say, "Oh, look, I notice I'm thinking about…"

Quick Review

- Thoughts aren't reality

  - You can have a negative thought one second and be in a completely different place the next

- Strong emotions don't make thoughts any more or any less true

- Simply observe your thoughts

  - If there are self-judgments, observe those, too

  - Use the exact phrase or something similar to, "Oh, look, I notice I'm thinking about..."

- Consider your mind as a tool to pursue what matters to you rather than deriving your identity from your mind

- If you have a thought you don't like, simply reset and go again

- The mental act of observing is all it takes

Self-Love Experiment #2
Do Something that Calls Out to You

There's something that's been calling out to you. It's time to trust and follow your inner voice.

This experiment isn't about making major life changes such as quitting your job or doing a year-long trip overseas. Although those may potentially be the best decisions for you, this activity isn't about that. This experiment is about expressing your heart and soul. Let's look at a few examples.

One spring, I wrote a poem about the lush greenness of the trees and grass. When I saw the beauty of the new life sprouting up all around, there was a longing in me to express what I felt about it. In other words, a longing called out to me and I expressed it through poetry. This past Christmas, I spent some time decorating our mantle in the living room because it seemed like a fun way to express creativity. Lastly, I haven't acted on this yet, but I have a longing to learn how to play a drum set, guitar, or another instrument. There's an awareness that musical expression is calling out to me.

For you, this could be a poem, piece of art, garden, learning an instrument, or decorating your living room. It could be a cooking class, improv group, or a new craft. Whatever it is, approach it with an attitude of expression and experimentation. This isn't about doing it well or being world-class at it. Again, it's strictly about expression of the longing that's within you.

Self-Love Experiment #2, Continued
Do Something that Calls Out to You

What is it that calls to you? Make a "date" with your own soul and enjoy expressing it. Remember, following through and keeping the date with yourself builds trust and therefore self-love.

Notes

Step 4

The Silver Bullet Formula
Separating Thoughts from Feelings

"Wholeness is not achieved by cutting off a portion of one's being,
but by integration of the contraries." -Carl Jung

Mixing thoughts and feelings is a dangerous thing. When we do it, there's no way out.

"Now wait a minute, Nic, I'm going to stop you there. You're mixing your thoughts and feelings." I used to get upset and offended when Ron would interrupt me about this. I'd be in midsentence, and he'd interrupt me. I thought the entire thoughts vs. feelings concept was a small matter of semantics.

Who cares if I say, "I *feel* like I'm never going to get better?" That's how people talk in our society! We say, "I feel like this" and "I feel like that" and then we say the thing we feel like. That's how it goes.

"You're giving your power away when you say that. You have no way out."

It didn't jive with me. It seemed like he was being rude and interrupting me for something that didn't matter. Of course, it did matter, and when this finally clicked for me, everything changed. Yes, this is very much an *inside* job. You may think it's the outside stuff, people, and circumstances that is the problem. It's not; it's the way you perceive those things. When the way you perceive those things changes, everything becomes renewed for you. The way you change how you perceive the outer things is through changing yourself on the inside. That's what learning to love yourself is all about: changing yourself on the inside.

In our society, we say "I feel like..." a lot. It's a widely accepted norm. The issue is that when it comes to ditching self-hatred and learning to love yourself, it's a huge trap.

Remember my story from earlier about the internal alarms going off every time my voice didn't operate properly? Let's look closely so you can see the real danger of mixing thoughts with feelings. As we go through this, remember that all of this takes place within milliseconds.

> First, my voice didn't function how I wanted. Immediately, I had the thought, "I'm weird and an outcast."
>
> Second, the thought of being weird and an outcast led to feelings of fear, anxiety, and frustration.
>
> Third, I would have another thought about how I'll never be able to connect with people and how life will always be miserable.
>
> Fourth, such thoughts led to more intense feelings of fear, anxiety, and frustration.
>
> Fifth, when I had the opportunity to talk with someone about this situation, I would say something like, "I feel like I'm a freak and like I'm never going to fit in."

What were the thoughts and what were the feelings in that example? The thoughts were, *I'll never be able to connect with people, I'm weird and an outcast*, and *life will always be miserable*. Next, what were the feelings? Fear, anxiety, and frustration. Feelings can be identified in a single word, whereas thoughts require multiple words.

When we don't distinguish between thoughts and feelings, we say convoluted things like, "I feel like I'm a freak." "Like I'm a freak" is a thought, not a feeling. The way to untangle that statement is by using this formula: [I think X] + [I feel Y about that]. X is the placeholder for the thought you'll plug into the formula, while Y is the placeholder for the feeling. It would look like this: [I think I'm a freak] + [I feel fear, anxiety, and frustration about that]. We're going to apply this formula to one of the most common (and most dangerous) thought-feeling traps people experience. Before doing that, let's specifically distinguish between what a thought is and what a feeling is.

Simply, a thought is something your mind thinks while a feeling is something your body feels. You cannot feel a thought. You cannot think a feeling.

Feelings entail a physiological sensation in the body. When you feel anger, there might be a burst of intensity down the midline of your chest to the gut. With sadness, there might be pressure in the chest that expands to the throat.

You have feelings *about* thoughts, but the thoughts are not in and of themselves feelings. In the above example, I said, "I feel like I'm a freak." "Freak" is not a feeling. Where does "freak" take place in terms of body sensation? It doesn't. A feeling *about* the thought "I'm a freak" takes place, absolutely. But freak is not itself a feeling.

Being concerned about finances, you might say, "I feel like I'm never going to have enough money." Is *I'm never going to have enough money* a feeling? Of course not; it's a thought. You do, however, have feelings *about* the thought that you're never going to have enough money. Likely, those feelings are fear, anxiety, and frustration. Below is a list of the most common unpleasant feelings. I'm not claiming that it's a complete list, but you can use it to identify 90% or more of the feelings you feel.

Three Primary Feelings:

1. Anger/Rage
2. Fear/Terror
3. Sadness/Grief

Four Combination Feelings:

1. Anxiety/Worry (fear projected into the future)
2. Frustration (anger + fear + anxiety)
3. Depression (sadness or anger turned inward [instead of expressed])
4. Shame (sadness + fear)

Two important notes:

I) Embarrassment and humiliation are variations of the feeling of shame.

II) Guilt: Healthy guilt takes place when you've done something wrong, hurtful, or harmful. Feeling "guilty" for something that wasn't wrong, e.g., appropriately setting a boundary at work or with a family member, is not guilt, it's shame.

What I wanted to know was, why does this matter? Either way, I'm still not doing too well whether I distinguish the thought from the feeling or not. Here's why: It matters because thoughts can endlessly recycle themselves while feelings are limited when singled out.

A pure feeling will run its course and fizzle out. Attaching thoughts to feelings, on the other hand, continuously triggers the feeling over and over, eventually leaving you completely exhausted. There's simply no way out of "I feel like a freak" or "I feel like I'll never have enough money." On the other hand, when you know how to treat your body as a <u>container</u> and *allow* feelings to run through it, which you'll learn in the next step, you'll never be stuck again.

Earlier, I mentioned that we'd work through a common and deadly thought-feeling trap. Let's do that now.

I feel trapped. Or, sometimes, *I feel like I'm trapped*. Have you ever said this about a situation? I know I used to, and it never led to progress. This trap ruins lives everywhere because it leaves people believing that they're helpless. This is how to break free.

First, let's recall the formula: [I think X] + [I feel Y about that]. In this example, what is the thought? The thought is, *I'm trapped*. Plug it in, like this: [I think I'm trapped] + [I feel Y about that].

Next, what's the feeling? It depends on the person. As I recall believing I was trapped in life, I often felt angry, fearful, frustrated, and depressed. Plug those feelings in: [I feel angry, fearful, frustrated, and depressed about that].

Putting the formula together, we have: [I think I'm trapped] + [I feel angry, fearful, frustrated, and depressed about that]. Now, as a completed sentence: I *think* I'm trapped and I *feel* angry, fearful, frustrated, and depressed about that.

To simplify this, whenever you say, "I feel like…" whatever follows will be the thought to plug into the formula. Then, look at the list of feelings above to identify the true feeling.

Again, why does this matter? When you can single out a feeling and deflate it, which you'll learn next, the thought is rendered harmless. Remember, thoughts are only powerful when they're supported by strong emotions. Single the emotion out, deflate it, and you're home free.

The Silver Bullet Process

Once you've separated the thought from the feeling, it's game over. Your feelings only have power over you when they remain wrapped up in endless thought cycles. This is a 3-part process, and you can begin in one of two ways.

Part 1

   a. This is the quickest way to freedom. Notice yourself having a negative thought (e.g., *I'm a loser*) or saying, "I feel like…" That's it. Noticing completes part-1 of this process.

   b. This way isn't as energy efficient, but it'll still save you from an avalanche. If you didn't notice the initial negative thought or when you said *I feel like…*, then notice that you're experiencing intensely uncomfortable emotions. They are a sign that you've identified with the thought in your head and then went through a cycle or two of supporting the thought with feelings and supporting the feelings with more negative thoughts.

Part 2

Identify the thought and plug it into the formula. If you say, *I feel like he doesn't care about me*, plug "I think he doesn't care about me" into the formula.

Part 3

Identify the feeling and plug it into the formula. Using the above example, what are your feelings *about* thinking that you're not cared about? Those feelings are the silver bullet because once you know what to do with them, which you'll learn in the next step, it takes the mystery out of handling these situations.

A Brief Note from the Author

I love to hear from readers.

Don't hesitate to send me an email at nic@nicsaluppo.com to tell me what's on your mind. Share what has stuck out to you about this book. Send me your favorite quotes and ideas. How has this book helped you? What burning questions still remain for you? Let me know!

And now, back to our regularly scheduled programming.

The Psychological Mechanism Behind
Separating Thoughts and Feelings

I used to be terrified of depression and anxiety. I was also terrified of being terrified. It was quite an emotional pickle. Learning the silver bullet formula got me out.

As explained, thoughts feed feelings and feelings feed thoughts. The issue is that most people don't realize it as it's happening. They're powerless over it because it's one big mish-mosh. I compare this to me analyzing an NBA team vs. Michael Jordan analyzing that team.

When I watch footage, I see people tossing a ball around and running back and forth near the hoop. They must be doing something meaningful, but I'm not sure exactly what that is, and I don't especially care to learn. On the other hand, Jordan sees the subtle things my eyes miss, like misdirection cues and nonverbal communication among teammates. Similarly, there is a process behind what leads to self-hatred and loathing, and that process involves jumbled thoughts and feelings. Until now, you simply haven't had the eye to be able to pick that process apart. The silver bullet exposes those thoughts and feelings, giving you the power to intervene.

Daily, I would get trapped in cycles of hating myself because I didn't understand the process behind what got me into the state of self-hatred and loathing. By not letting me get away with saying *I feel like...* Ron empowered me to break out of these cycles. All that was left was learning what to do with the feelings once I had them singled out.

Quick Review

- Mixing thoughts and feelings is dangerous because thoughts will ceaselessly fuel more feelings

- Singling out a feeling is empowering because once you know what to do with it, you can deflate it

- The silver bullet formula for separating thoughts and feelings is: [I think X] + [I feel Y about that]

- As soon as you notice yourself saying "I feel like..." view it as a red flag and plug it into the formula

Self-Love Experiment #3
Be a Loving Parent to Yourself

Being a loving parent to yourself means giving yourself the love you wanted but didn't receive. We all crave and need love, but not many realize that we can give this love to ourselves. Learning to give this love to yourself is the pinnacle of adult emotional maturation because it gives us self-sustaining emotional security and prevents us from seeking parental love where it can't be found, like through a partner, friend, job, group, therapist, clergy person, or anyplace else.

If you wanted someone to hold you and say, "It's okay," or "I love you," you can do this for yourself by visualizing the adult you holding the toddler, child, teenage, or younger adult you. Your brain can't tell the difference between emotions experienced when visualizing this vs. the physical experience, which is why it can create deep and lasting emotional healing.

So, ask yourself: How do I need to be loved? The options are endless, but to give you a few ideas, here are several that have been powerful for myself, fellow journeyers, and clients:

- Give myself permission to be playful.
- Give myself permission to have feelings, including anger, grief, shame, and fear.
- I need to let myself know that I'm here for myself, emotionally speaking.
- I need to say *I'm sorry* to myself for rejecting myself.

Self-Love Experiment #3, Continued
Be a Loving Parent to Yourself

- I need to go back to a specific emotionally harmful incident from my past and visualize my adult self protecting the helpless child I was.
- I want to write or speak aloud warm, kind words to myself like, "I love you," "It's okay," or, "I'm here for you."

As you do this experiment, it's important you view this as one part of you giving love to another part of you. This is a book about integration and wholeness. Giving the love you never received from your parents to yourself removes the need to demand (maybe unconsciously) that the world around you – spouse, children, friends, associates – give you that love. Giving this love to yourself creates emotional stability and security in addition to emotionally relating to others as a mutual adult.

Notes

Step 5

Firing the Silver Bullet
What to do with Feelings

"The sorrow which has no vent in tears
may make other organs weep." -Henry Maudsley
(Quote taken from *The Divided Mind*, by John E. Sarno, M.D.)

n the last section, you learned how to separate intertwined thoughts and feelings. If wrangling a feeling seems similar to a one v. one showdown with a grizzly bear, don't worry, you're not alone.

Most of us are afraid of our feelings. We're *trained* to be afraid of them before we're old enough to decide for ourselves. As discussed earlier in the book, when we're shamed for our feelings or told that our feelings aren't okay – either directly or indirectly – we learn to fear them. They're not okay because they mean a) something's wrong with us, and b) our caregivers will withdraw love and attention.

As a young man, I struggled terribly with the belief I was sensitive. I concluded this because I compared myself to someone who displayed a macho persona. It wasn't until later that I realized the macho persona was actually a way of keeping his own feelings repressed. Beneath the external shell was a lot of insecurity and fear.

Due to believing that having feelings meant I was sensitive, not tough, or otherwise unmanly, I was afraid of the feelings. Not only that, I was also afraid of what I perceived to be the pain of feelings. Once you let them flow, they never stop, right? It's normal to think that some people can feel their feelings, but for you, it's different. For you, your feelings are so strong that it would lead to a never-ending waterfall that will drown the entire earth or a rage attack that will destroy every living thing.

We like to think our feelings are too big to handle as an additional defense against feeling them. You can handle your feelings, and once you learn how you'll be able to love even the parts of yourself that have feelings. What an enormous breakthrough that will be.

`\\\\ \\\\`

During undergrad at the age of 21, I remember lying in bed, thinking I needed psychological help. I also remember choosing to suffer in silence over asking for help. The message I was taught growing up, more so through modeling than verbally, was that having feelings meant I wasn't a man. Or, if I was still a man, I was a wimpy version of one. So, rather than seeking help, I chose to "be a man" and continue quietly suffering.

If I could go back and talk to my 21-year old self, I would teach him the 4 Truths about Feelings:

1. Feelings are natural
2. Feelings are neither good nor bad
3. It's much healthier to learn to work with feelings than repress them
4. One of the most valuable life skills you can learn is letting feelings run through you

`\\\\ \\\\`

Learning what to do with feelings, especially unpleasant ones, is essential in learning to love yourself again. To learn what to do with them, you must first grasp the 4 Truths about Feelings.

Truth 1: Feelings are natural. Everybody has them, even the toughest men and strongest women out there. Having feelings makes you just like everybody else. The difference is that most people learn to hide their feelings. It's all right to have feelings, and yours are perfectly okay.

Truth 2: Feelings are neither good nor bad. Feelings are part of the human experience. Shame and fear are not bad, they're just unpleasant. Likewise, sadness and anger are not bad, but they can be painful. Be careful not to confuse unpleasant or painful with bad. Having an unpleasant feeling does not indicate something is wrong with you any more than waking up in the morning with a full, uncomfortable bladder indicates something is wrong with you.

Truth 3: It's much healthier to learn to work with feelings than repress them. Repressing your feelings creates more pain. I hope you'll decide to process and express them, which we will learn in a moment. Not giving your emotions the chance to express themselves creates physical tension and emotional weight you've got to carry around for the rest of your life.

Truth 4: One of the most valuable life skills you can learn is letting feelings run through you. Emotions don't go anywhere. They stay in the body until dissolved through expression. Not being consciously aware of your feelings doesn't signify that they're gone; it only signifies that you're not currently aware of them. To exemplify this, sit quietly on the couch for one hour. Just you and the couch – no music, headphones, phone, or anything else. Most people fear spending time completely alone with no distractions. The reason for this is *fear of the feelings* which are normally kept at bay through distractions. Letting feelings run through you is a vitally important life skill because you learn to no longer be afraid of your feelings as they arise throughout life. And make no mistake, they *will* arise, so it pays to not be afraid of them.

Having an emotion is never unhealthy; rather, avoiding emotions is what creates a lack of health because they create physical, emotional, and mental tension when not expressed. The next step is learning exactly how to handle them when they arise.

゛゛゛ ゛゛゛

We've all heard of someone who has had an emotional blowup or breakdown.

Blowing up refers to someone with an uncontrollable outburst of anger. One client was driving with her boyfriend in Atlanta, GA, to visit her parents' new home. Neither of them had been to Atlanta, and her boyfriend was having trouble navigating the crazy traffic. He made a wrong turn and just like that, she blew up. Things came out of her mouth that she'd never said out loud before. When it was all over, she could hardly believe it was her who had said those things. *Why did I do that*? she asked me.

Breaking down refers to an experience of uncontrollable grief. My clients will often describe this experience by saying, *I was so emotional and for no reason*. They might say something like, *I don't cry, but I just couldn't hold it back. Why did this happen?*

The same mechanism is at play in both cases: emotional pressure. If you avoid, suppress, repress, or otherwise shove down your feelings, the pressure's going to build. A single playing card in a 52 card deck weighs about 0.06 ounces. Yet, it's that single card that brings down the entire house of cards. Or, if you prefer, it's the one piece of straw that broke the camel's back.

Similarly, when your emotions have been building up over months, years, or multiple decades, that one final card or piece of straw can set you off. When someone says, "I don't cry," what they really mean is, "I don't cry because I hold my feelings down." When the nicest person you've ever met has a rage-filled blowup and they say, "But I never get angry," what they really mean is, "I never get angry because I shove it deep down inside of me."

The key is to view your emotions as moving energy forms and your body as a *container* for the energy to move through. When you learn this skill, you'll never again need to be afraid of your feelings.

Make Your Body a Container
for Emotions to Flow Through

This method is a tool for both handling feelings as they arise throughout the day and for dissolving emotional wounds from the past. In learning to love yourself, addressing both is important.

When I started the inner healing journey, my mentor, Dan, talked a lot about feeling your feelings. The idea started making sense, so I thought I'd try it out with a breakup I was going through. I was 24 at the time and feeling upset about it.

That night, instead of distracting myself through reading or TV, I decided to feel my feelings. Lying on my back, I stopped thinking about it and got in touch with the physical sensations of the feelings in my body. I felt an intensity expand in my gut, solar plexus, and heart. I didn't add any narration or commentary using my mind – I felt the pure feeling.

It was neither particularly comfortable nor uncomfortable. They were just sensations in my body. The discomfort comes only when we attach thoughts to the feeling. The feelings in my body pulsated intensely for a minute or two, then gradually reduced in intensity and finally dissolved completely. That night I fell asleep faster, slept more soundly, and woke up more refreshed than usual. Taking an emotional load off can work wonders. It's my secret method for falling asleep.

When I'm having trouble sleeping, I don't say, "Well, I just can't sleep because my mind won't shut off." Instead, I say, "My mind is hyperactive because there's a feeling beneath the thoughts that needs to run its course." It could be anger, fear, shame, or grief – it doesn't matter which feeling it is because, when separated from thoughts, they're *all* just physiological sensations in the body. I can't tell you how often, once I got in touch with the feeling in my body, I was asleep within 30 seconds. *Unexpressed emotions create internal tension and hyperactive thoughts. Feeling those feelings relieves that tension.*

Container Method Process

Turning your body into a container for feelings to flow through requires two parts.

1. Taking your attention away from your thoughts and bringing it into your body.

2. Allowing the feelings to flow through you.

Taking your attention away from your thoughts and bringing it into your body. We've talked a lot about not giving so much importance to your thoughts. It's so important because it frees you to let your emotions run their course through your body, resulting in reduced tension and anxiety as well as a relaxation response.

Pinching the skin on the back of your arm would create a stinging sensation in your body. Similarly, performing a certain number of bodyweight squats would create a burning sensation in your legs. The same is true of your emotions, it's just that you're not used to looking for the sensation.

The main areas of your body where you're going to feel emotions are in the 5 Hot Spots: 1) lower gut 2) belly 3) solar plexus 4) chest, and 5) throat. When starting out, place a hand on the 5 Hot Spots, spending 30 seconds on each area. Notice the physiological sensations in all five locations.

Initially, this requires a concentrated effort because your brain and body have habitually blocked these emotions since before you were self-aware enough to know that was happening. Your natural reaction may be to reach for your phone, the remote, a snack, an activity, or, if you're like most of us, your mind will offer endless commentary. The commentary is a defense mechanism that prevents you from feeling, so stick with the physical sensation and don't get roped in by your thoughts no matter how seductive they are.

Allowing the feelings to flow through you. This is it. You're here. Learning to love yourself means loving all of yourself, including your feelings. Feelings aren't meant to be fought, squashed, or shoved away. If you did those things to a person, your relationship with that person wouldn't be good at all. As people, we want the freedom to be who we are. We want to be accepted by others for who we are. Similarly, accept your feelings for what they are.

Truly, you don't have to do anything. Just allow your feelings to flow. They will naturally flow once you stop clinging to your thoughts, as thoughts are the defense mechanism that prevents you from actively being with your feelings.

You might notice intensity expanding from your heart up into your throat or from your gut and then into your chest. Whatever it is, it's all okay. Allow it to happen. The intensity will increase for 30 seconds to a few minutes, and then there will be a pulsating sensation which gradually slows and eventually dissolves completely.

Allowing means noticing the physical sensation without placing commentary, meaning, or thoughts onto it. It simply is. You simply are. Uncomfortable does not mean bad.

You might have the urge to cry or shout, and that's okay too if you're alone or with safe, nonjudgmental people. I don't recommend doing this if children are within earshot as they don't have the capacity to interpret it in a healthy way. Their primal minds may view it as danger or crisis.

I recommend using your newfound relationship with your own feelings to nurture your children's feelings – remember, they're just physiological sensations. It's okay for your kids to have feelings. You don't have to make them feel better nor do you need to make them stop; just be present while they feel. They'll get it out and then move on as if all is well...and all truly *is well* because they were able to unload emotional weight. Unloading Emotional Weight = Great. Children only need correction when they're expressing feelings in a disrespectful way (name-calling, sarcasm) or in a way that physically harms others or property. Remember, the only reason parents are uncomfortable with their children's feelings is because the parents are uncomfortable with their own feelings. Let them have their big feelings and play the role of guiding them in safely expressing those feelings.

The Psychological Mechanism Behind Letting Feelings Flow

Letting feelings flow is like opening a release valve. It decreases pressure within the container. Here, you are the container. When you don't open the release valve, emotions build up and the container eventually breaks in the form of a blowup or breakdown.

Your anxiety, depression, self-hatred, and self-loathing all stem from battling your feelings instead of letting them flow. It's difficult to avoid feeling depressed and therefore stop hating yourself when you have months, years, or decades of stored up feelings in you.

If you don't drain an infection, it hurts more and more. But when you drain the pus, you experience relief, and your emotions work the same way. Always keep Step 4, the silver bullet, in mind because this all hinges on your ability to avoid the trap of mixing thoughts and feelings.

Keeping emotions locked inside of you takes energy even when you're not aware of them. I used to take 3-hour naps regularly because I was habitually and unconsciously blocking my feelings. Once I let them flow through me, I couldn't take a 3-hour nap if I tried because I was no longer using so much energy to keep them locked down.

Quick Review

- In many families and as a society in general, we're trained to be afraid of our feelings before we can understand what's happening. There's nothing to be afraid of as they're simply physiological sensations.

- The 4 Truths about Feelings:

    o They're natural – everybody has them.

    o They're neither good nor bad – unpleasant feelings don't indicate something is wrong with you.

    o It's healthier to work with feelings than repress or avoid them because working with them relieves emotional pressure and creates inner peace.

    o Letting feelings flow through you is a skill you can learn.

- Blowing up and breaking down are caused by the same mechanism: the pressure of unexpressed feelings.

- The discomfort of feelings comes when we attach meaning and negative thoughts to them. Without these thoughts, they're simply physiological sensations.

- There are two parts to making your body into a container that feelings can flow through:

    o First, take your attention away from your thoughts and bring it to your body.

    o Second, once you've contacted a feeling, notice it and allow it to flow.

Notes

Step 6

Putting It All Together

W e've done a lot of zooming in on specific areas that will help you learn to love yourself again. Now, it's time to zoom back out to see how they all work together. This section will help you understand the larger perspective of working these steps.

We started with learning that self-hatred is a combination of frustration plus harsh self-judgments. In understanding this, you can end self-hatred through a) having a method for dissolving emotions, and b) having a method for rendering thoughts harmless. Once this happens, loving yourself, which is a state of being warm and welcoming towards yourself, becomes natural.

Equipped with an understanding of how self-hatred forms, we then discussed the two necessary prerequisites to succeed in learning to love yourself again. They are 1) understanding that a lack of self-love is not natural, and 2) avoiding the trap of an all-or-nothing mindset. Not loving yourself is learned, and it typically happens at an age before you're aware of what you're being taught. By the time you're old enough to consciously think, it has already become a part of you, which is why you haven't questioned it until now.

Avoiding the all-or-nothing mindset is vital because it's deadly. There will be "slips" when you get caught up in frustration and self-judgment again. It's okay. Once you're aware of what has happened, simply continue moving forward with your steps and tools.

With the right mindset in place, it's time for Step 1. This step is all about not fighting against your initial upset to avoid the Double

Arrow. When you're upset about being upset or try to fight against being upset, that's like firing a second arrow at yourself. It exacerbates your feelings, making the situation mentally and emotionally worse.

In Step 2, you shift away from the "inner" work and look at the 4 Cornerstone Habits that people who love themselves utilize. These are eating when you're hungry (and planning ahead to have enough food if you're out for the day), drinking plenty of water, using the bathroom when you need to go, and offering plenty of time for your body to rest. This step comes early in the process because implementing concrete ways of loving yourself is a great way to build momentum. Treating yourself in loving ways before you have the emotion-based and thought-based steps and tools completely dialed in will always keep you on track.

Getting back to the internal work, you learned about not identifying with your thoughts in Step 3. If your mind is a tool for pursuing the things that are worthwhile and meaningful to you, your mind will sometimes misfire in that pursuit. It's okay. Misfires are normal – reset and move ahead. You don't have to believe your thoughts. Choose the ones that support your greatest goals while discarding the others.

The reality that you don't have to believe your thoughts was exemplified when I showed you examples of what my mind told me over and over, yet reality proved my thoughts wrong. If a thought doesn't support your purpose, count it as a misfire. If it does, go with it. But know that you choose whether to follow a thought or not.

You've ceased fighting against the initial upset and learned that thoughts don't need to be automatically agreed with. These two steps alone have freed up a lot of space and energy in you. You're now ready for the silver bullet in Step 4: separating thoughts from feelings. Do you remember why this is the silver bullet? When you can single a feeling out, you can dissolve it. However, if a feeling is jumbled and tangled up with a thought, "I feel like you don't love me," for example, there's no escaping. The thought continuously fuels the feeling and the feeling continuously fuels the thought, leaving you drained and exhausted. By singling out the feeling, you stop the downward spiral. The formula for this is: [I think X] + [I feel Y about that].

You've singled the feeling out, and now it's time to learn what to do with that feeling in Step 5. This is where you fire the silver bullet. As a reminder, remember that self-hatred is frustration + harsh self-judgments. Without the feelings, the self-judgments would mean nothing. Similarly, without the self-judgments, the feelings wouldn't seem so bad. You've already learned what to do with the self-judgments (i.e., thoughts) in Steps 1, 3, and 4. Now, it's time to dissolve the feelings.

This step comes last due to the necessary foundational work. Handling emotions can be tricky without the groundwork that came before this step. Plus, we're trained in our society to fear our emotions. Self-hatred is difficult to break free of because you're fighting, kicking, and scratching against your emotions, which are a part of yourself. In this step, you learned to get in touch with feelings and allow them to flow by noticing the physiological sensations in your body. When you're no longer afraid of or fighting against your feelings, it's very difficult for self-hatred to make a home for itself. It *requires* the environment of thrashing and kicking against your emotions. When you stop doing that, self-hatred can't survive.

Self-Love Experiment #4
Uncover a Valuable Lesson for Yourself

People who love themselves can learn from mistakes, whereas people who don't love themselves have difficulty learning from mistakes.

Have you ever met someone who would never admit they were wrong or say, "I'm sorry"? It's not anything against you; it's the difference between someone with self-love and someone without it. When you don't love yourself, admitting a mistake is equal to saying, "I am a piece of garbage who doesn't deserve to exist." A mistake isn't just a mistake, it's a total, all-encompassing, final judgment about who you are at the deepest level.

When you love yourself, though, you love not only your good performances but your mistakes. You give yourself space to learn from them. For example, I want to be a connected, loving husband to my wife. However, are there times when I direct an ugly side of myself towards her? Of course. When this happens, I thank her for telling me how she felt about it and look inward with honesty. I might say, "My intentions weren't good. What I did was wrong." When it happens the other way around, she does the same thing for me.

Because we openly admit to one another when we were wrong, our connection grows deeper all the time. On the other hand, I see many clients who haven't admitted to their own mistakes in the relationship. They don't know how to communicate their feelings without being critical, and they become defensive when the other person expresses concerns about the relationship. These are two telltale signs of a person who hasn't learned to love themselves.

Self-Love Experiment #4, Continued
Uncover a Valuable Lesson for Yourself

Give yourself the gift of growth. Where have you harmed someone? It's okay to identify it – it speaks volumes to your willingness to grow. You don't have to judge your entire self as unworthy, terrible, or a piece of trash. You are singling out an event and using it as an opportunity for self-reflection, not placing judgment on yourself as an entire individual.

Notes

One Last Thing

Did you know that a review from you makes a huge difference? It's true.

It makes a difference in the lives of others. Most people choose books based on reviews, and if another human being is in need of learning to love themselves, leaving your review helps them find this book to bring them hope and encouragement.

We've all had the experience of buying a life-changing book based on the review of a person who we'll never meet.

With reviews, just one sentence about how this book benefited you is more than enough, and it can be completed in less than 60 seconds. It's easy—simply go to the product page of this book and scroll down until you see a button that says "Write a customer review". Click the button, and from there, it's a user-friendly, fast, and easy process.

Read Next

Outsmart Negative Thinking

Simple Mindfulness Methods to Control Negative Thoughts, Stop Anxiety, & Finally Experience Happiness

Can negative thinking be stopped? Is there a solution, or do you just have to live with it?

Just as there are effective methods when it comes to gardening, woodworking, cooking, and weightlifting, so too are there effective techniques when it comes to thinking. All it takes is a little bit of mindfulness, and you can successfully learn how to think so that negative thinking and anxiety can no longer overtake your life and torture you.

Once you learn these methods, negative thinking and anxiety will go from seeming like an overwhelming tidal wave to an annoying little fly you can easily shoo away.

Outsmart Negative Thinking is available on Amazon.

Appendix A: Identity

"If I'm not my thoughts, then who am I?" is a common and natural question to ask. Before beginning this discussion, know that it's going to be brief, as this falls out of the scope of this book.

The short answer to the above question is this: I don't know, and I don't find it helpful to try and figure it out, either. You would do much, much better to focus on experiencing life deeply as opposed to figuring out who you are, as who you are is always changing. That's why I say I simply am. I'm neither amazing nor unamazing. I simply am.

There's a saying that goes something like, "You are not your thoughts. You are the one who witnesses your thoughts." That's great, but who is the one, then, who witnesses your thoughts? This is why I encourage you to not worry too much about this question.

Here's the thing. I couldn't tell you exactly who I am, but I know a few things. I know that something calls me from within to spread the good news of emotional healing. This "call" seems to transcend "me." I know it's there, but I couldn't tell you how it got there or where it came from.

I suspect it has something to do with God. Personally, I believe in God and I believe that God's spirit stirs in our souls and inclines us towards meaningful work. Christ spoke a lot about love, gentleness, peace, joy, and abundance. So, somehow, I believe Christ's spirit stirs and calls me—note that this is what I personally believe.

I'm aware that talk of God and Christ can elicit memories of bad experiences in many people. I'm not the type of Christ-follower to sit here and judge you. My only job is to love you and help you love yourself. So, if you've had negative experiences relating to church or you find yourself in the position of being atheist or agnostic, know that I don't speak about Christ and God from the all-too-common perspective of being hateful and judgmental. I'm also not going to apologize for my faith—I promised a short discussion on identity, and this subject plays a role in that discussion. With that said, given how certain groups have been hated and shunned within the church, I do want to make it abundantly clear that I'm not going to hate and judge you simply because you don't think and believe exactly as I do.

Returning to the subject matter of identity, if God is God, then God is infinite. Therefore, I can understand evermore about God, but will never completely understand how God operates on this side of existence, and it would be futile to try. I'd much rather spend my time and energy on simply existing and following the stirrings inside of me that seem to call me to a meaningful life.

Coming full circle, who are you, if not your thoughts? I would say to focus on what calls you and stirs you from deep within, but don't focus too much on creating an etched in stone answer. As you continue to grow and gain wisdom, how you see yourself will constantly change, so what's the point in coming up with a hardline definition?

You can identify things and qualities that are important to you, but those aren't who you are, either. They're decisions and ways of life, but if they were stripped away, what would be left?

Further, knowing exactly who you are is not necessary for learning to love yourself. It's enough to know that your thoughts aren't true and that your feelings are okay. I can't tell you exactly who I am, but I know that I'm drawn to live out a certain purpose, and to me, that's enough. Figuring out who I am has never brought fulfillment, but living out a purpose has. Grow daily, know that you're loved and not condemned by Christ (to the person saying, "Certainly not me," yes, even you), and follow your soul's calling. Whatever you do, don't get sucked into the black hole of trying to answer a question in which the answer itself is always evolving and in which the answer can be understood in infinite ways. Trust what calls to you in your soul.

Get in Touch

There are a few ways to get in touch:

Join my email list at www.nicsaluppo.com and receive the eBook *The Five Laws of Emotional Resilience* as a bonus when you join.

Email me at nic@nicsaluppo.com.

Find me on Instagram at the handle @nicsaluppo.

Made in the USA
Coppell, TX
17 March 2023

14387555R00069